To Ryan
With lots of love
Paula Elliott

EVERY DAY CAN FEEL LIKE CHRISTMAS

JUST COLOR YOUR WORLD WITH LOVE

By

Paula Elliott

Illustrations by

Sandy Royall

Planetary Publications
P.O. Box 66
Boulder Creek, CA 95006

Published in the United States of America by:
Planetary Publications
14795 West Park Ave., Boulder Creek, California 95006
(800)-372-3100 (408) 338-2161

Manufactured in the United States of America by Baker-Johnson

Library of Congress Cataloging In Publication Data

Elliott, Paula
Every day can feel like Christmas: just color your world with love / story by Paula Elliott : illustrations by Sandy Royall.
p. cm.
Summary: Children talking to Santa learn to spread the joy of Christmas by loving people every day.
ISBN 1-879052-02-4: $4.95
[1. Christmas — Fiction.] I. Royall, Sandy, Ill. II. Title.
PZ7.E458Ev 1991
91-9718
CIP
AC

10 9 8 7 6 5 4 3 2 1

This book is dedicated to Mom and Dad, and all my buddies, with heartfelt thanks for teaching me, by their example, that the most important gift you can give someone is the gift of love.

This story is also dedicated to Lew Childre, who really is "Santa Claus" to anyone fortunate enough to meet him. He has helped me to understand and use the power of my own heart, which brings me ever deeper levels of love for people, and an ever wider appreciation for life. Thank you, Lew — my days really do feel like Christmas!

May all of you who read this book have the fun of discovering how wonderful your own heart is, as you give your gifts of love to the people around you.

P.E.

Once upon a time, it was a beautiful Christmas Eve. All over the world, people were wrapping their gifts, picking up family members at airports, decorating their houses and Christmas trees, baking Christmas cookies...all the final preparations to be ready to enjoy one of their most favorite times of the year —Christmas Eve and Christmas Day.

Each boy and girl, mom and dad, brother and sister had their own reasons for loving this time of year, but all the reasons added up to the same thing: Christmas is a time when people's hearts feel happy — families get together, and peace is felt throughout the world.

Of course, there is also the giving and receiving of gifts .... and the chance for everyone to express, through these gifts, how much they truly do love each other.

This particular Christmas Eve became special, different from any other, because of some big magic that took place in the people's hearts.

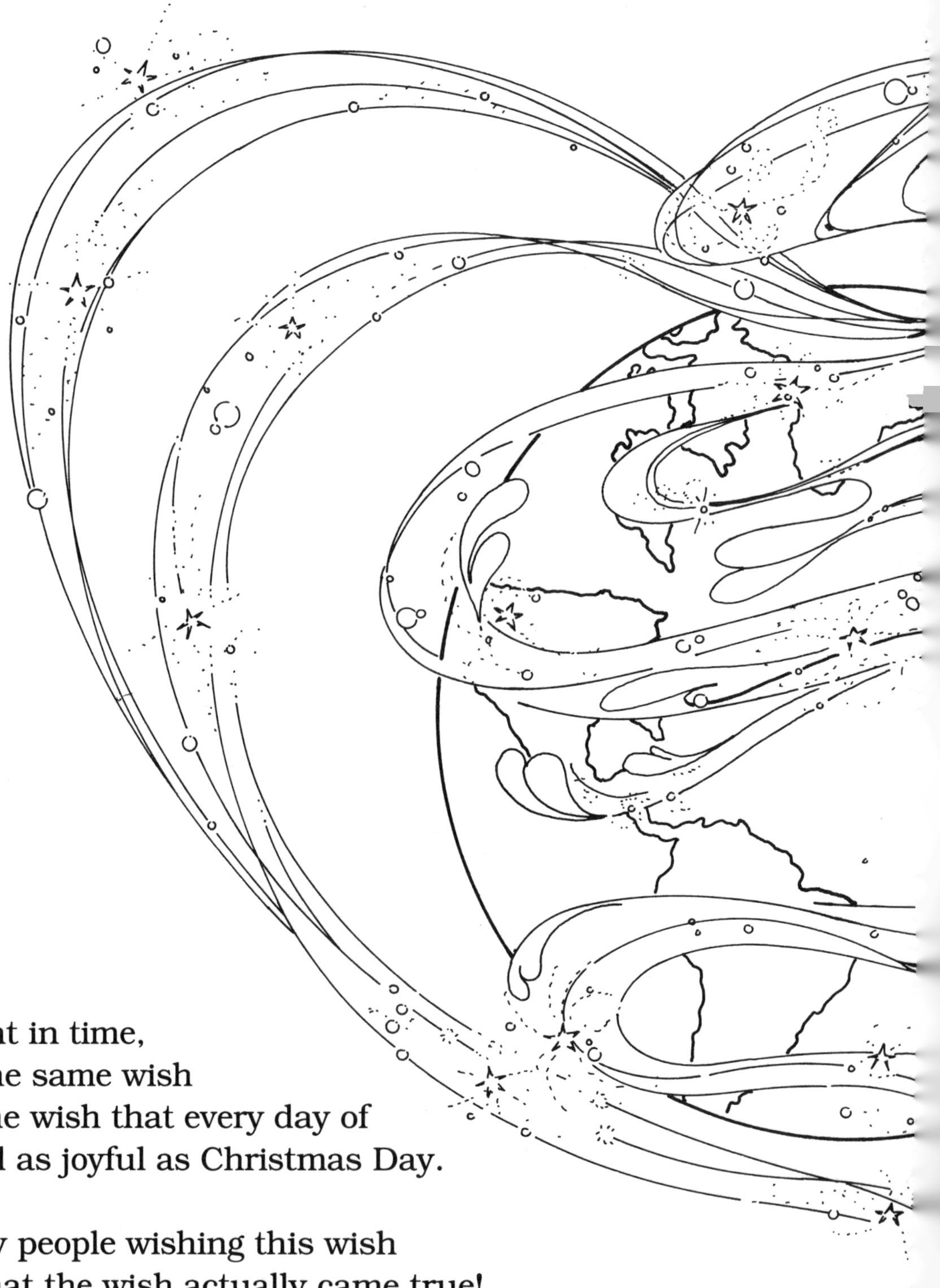

At the same moment in time,
many people had the same wish
in their hearts — the wish that every day of
their lives could feel as joyful as Christmas Day.

There were so many people wishing this wish
from their hearts that the wish actually came true!

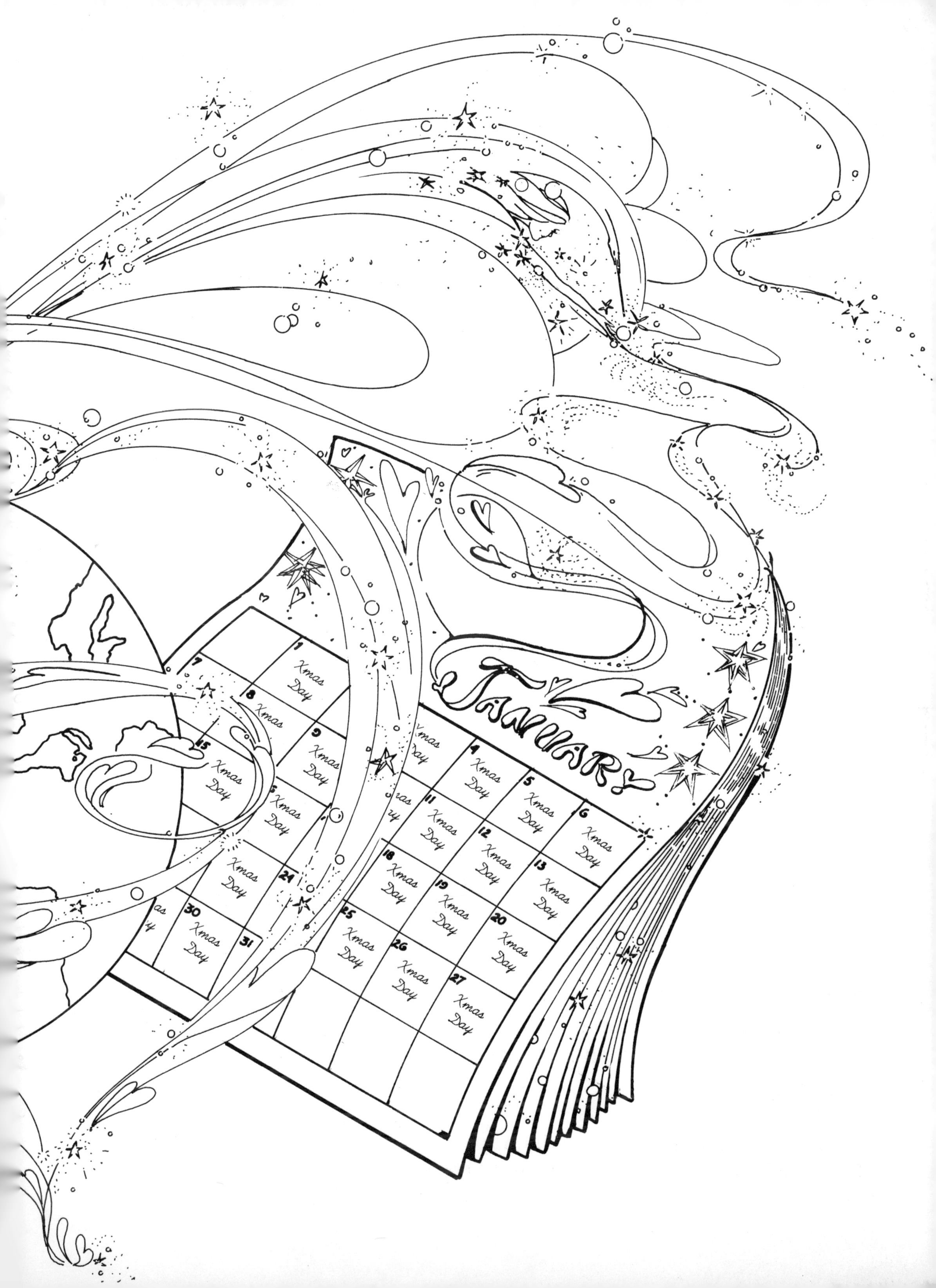
JANUARY
1
Xmas
Day
7
8
Xmas
15
Xmas
Day
9
Xmas
Day
4
Xmas
Day
5
Xmas
Day
6
Xmas
Day
11
Xmas
Day
12
Xmas
Day
13
Xmas
Day
18
Xmas
Day
19
Xmas
Day
20
Xmas
Day
24
25
Xmas
Day
26
Xmas
Day
27
Xmas
Day
30
Xmas
Day
31

JANUARY

On Christmas morning, people everywhere opened their gifts, and many people received calendars for the New Year. They were beautiful calendars, as always, but with one big difference: each day of the calendars was printed with the words, "Christmas Day!"

Now, you might think that since so many people had wished for this, much rejoicing would have followed the realization that every day of the next year was going to be Christmas Day, but no!

The first thing that the grown-up people did was to panic and begin to worry about all the details of what it would mean to have Christmas every day!

The fathers wondered, "How will I get my job done if every day of the year is a holiday?" The mailmen worried that they could never, ever deliver all the Christmas cards.

The mothers worried, "How could I possibly cook Christmas dinner every day of the year?" The gardeners were afraid they could never grow enough poinsettias or Christmas trees.

The grown-ups had one worry that was common among all of them — how could they ever find gifts for all their loved ones, every day for a whole year?

Only the children of the world were ready to celebrate, because for them, Christmas every day meant all fun days of play instead of school days, with a visit from Santa Claus every night! They were all sure they had made it to heaven!

A few days went by after Christmas, and the children realized that they could never have the kind of fun year they were hoping for if the grown-ups stayed in such a state of panic and worry.

So the children got together to figure out a way to help the grown-ups relax and have fun. The children decided to visit the only grown-up that would know what to do about a whole year of Christmases — Santa Claus!

The children were positive that since Santa Claus was so good at bringing Christmas joy to lots of people, he would surely know some helpful hints about how to handle having Christmas every day.

So a delegation of twenty five children, from all different countries, packed a lunch and put on their warmest clothes...

...and went to the North Pole to see Santa Claus!

They found him at home, drinking hot chocolate in a big, comfortable chair, reading a brand-new stack of children's letters telling what they wanted most for Christmas.

HOME
is
where the
Heart
dear
Santa

The children gathered close to him, on his lap and on the floor around him. They told him all about the coming year of Christmas Days, and the way that all the grown-ups were thinking and worrying.

When they finished their story, Santa Claus threw back his head and laughed, "Ho! Ho! Ho!   So, they finally got their greatest wish and now they don't know what to do about it! Ho! Ho! Ho!"

"Now, all the people of the world will get to learn what it is they *really* love about Christmas, and it will be you children that will teach the grown-ups!"

"But Santa, what do we teach them? How do we make them feel happy that every day is Christmas?" the children asked.

Santa said, "First, tell them to stop thinking about the details — dinners to cook, letters to mail, products to produce and sell — in fact, tell them to STOP THINKING, period!"

"Ask them to be quiet and listen to what their hearts were trying to tell them when they wished every day could be Christmas. Their hearts weren't wishing for a year of details and extra responsibilities!"

"Their hearts were wishing for a year full of days that *feel* like Christmas — days when you look around at all the ones you love, appreciate them, and express that appreciation and love through some sort of gift, or kiss, or hug or song."

"Tell the grown-ups that a whole year of Christmases is a gift for everyone, to be able to *forget* the details, the preparations, and the shopping! Then, you will be free to celebrate the love of Christmas time simply by giving gifts from the heart, and enjoying each moment of any day as if it were the most beautiful Christmas celebration."

"Let me give you some examples. Have any of you kids ever felt how happy it makes your mom feel when you offer to wash the dishes after dinner, or give her a painting you made at school, or just give her a surprise hug when she doesn't expect it?"

"Or, how about how good *you* feel when your family surprises you with your favorite food for dinner, or when someone helps you with the hardest part of your homework?"

"It's fun to give people the little things that you know would make their hearts happy, especially when you can surprise them and have them know that it came from your heart to their heart... ...not because it is a certain day of the year, but just because your heart wanted to tell them, 'I love you'."

"It's the 'I love you' coming from so many hearts at once that makes people love Christmas the way they do. So, if you children could all go home and spend the next year finding little ways to say 'I love you' to the people near to you, whoever they are, you will truly have a year where every day feels like Christmas."

"Some people, especially the grown-ups, will want to know how you learned to be so giving, and you can tell them all that I have said. Other people will just take your example of giving into their hearts, and without hearing any explanations, will know that what they want more than anything is to play this giving game *with* you, and find little ways to give to you."

"That's the way giving works — it makes someone's heart feel so good that the only way to say 'thank you' is to give back, to the original giver and to whoever comes your way."

Santa raised one eyebrow and asked, "Do you feel like you can go home and help all those worried grown-ups now?"

"Oh, yes! Thank you, Santa!" cheered the children.

Santa smiled and said, "Well, I want you to know that you all gave me a gift by coming to see me — I've never had so many smiling children in my lap and home all at once! I have a surprise I want to give you, but I have to get it ready."

"Mrs. Claus is in the kitchen baking cookies — why don't you all go join her while you wait for me?"

The children jumped up and ran to find Mrs. Claus. She was just finishing the baking, and they all pitched in and cleaned up the pans and the table before sitting down to enjoy cookies and hot chocolate with her.

As they were finishing the last cookie, they heard bells jingling outside. All the children scampered to the window just in time to see Santa Claus pull up his big, empty sleigh with all the reindeer ready to fly!

The children screamed with joy, and hurried to put their coats on and kiss Mrs. Claus goodbye.

Outside, Santa was waiting for them with a twinkle in his eye and the happiest smile they had ever seen. "Ho! Ho! Ho! Get in, all of you!" he cried. "I'm so glad you came all this way to see me that I wanted to give you the most adventuresome gift I could imagine. I'm going to deliver each one of you to your homes in my sleigh, and show you all my favorite sights along the way!"

The children arrived home bubbling with fun and their new stories about giving, and they helped all the grown-ups make the year of Christmas Days a year of giving, from heart to heart to heart to heart to heart...

THE END

Books, Tapes, and Games to Find Your Heart Treasures

Fluffy and Sparky: A Story about True Buddies, by Paula Elliott

Fluffy and Sparky is a delightful new children's story about two sea otters who both love to play, but each in their own way. Fluffy loves to play slowly, so she can appreciate the beauty of each moment. Sparky loves to go fast, so he can have as much fun and adventure as possible. When they meet, they realize that it might be more fun to play with a buddy, and in playing together, they learn a lesson about the fun to be found in surrendering "their way" of playing in order to love a buddy more. They discover a new way of playing that honors the preferences of both. A wonderful bedtime story for children of all ages, *Fluffy and Sparky* helps children find the wider heart and world that comes from surrendering to another's way of being his or her own true self.
$12.95, hardcover, 8 1/2" by 11", 32 pages, each page with outstanding color illustrations by Sandy Royall. For ages 3 and up.

The Crystal Lady, by Deborah Rozman

In this enchanting new storybook, Deborah Rozman introduces children to the magical world of the heart. Two schoolchildren, Cherie and her friend Davey, discover the value of an open heart as they face real-life challenges at school, with parents, and with siblings. They are introduced to their own inner "heart crystal" by the gentle wisdom of the lovely Crystal Lady. She shows them how to feel it and how to hold the special feeling in day-to-day life. She helps them with practical everyday problems that all children face, showing them a totally new way to turn upsets into positive experiences and turn bad days into fun ones by using their own inner heart power. During the course of the story, they gain self-confidence, self-esteem, security, become better buddies and discover how all relationships really can get better and better. Exquisitely illustrated with original watercolors by Sandy Royall, each copy of the book is packaged with a beautiful surprise gift from the Crystal Lady: a genuine clear quartz crystal.
$19.95, hardcover, 8" x 10", 72 pages, 30 full-color illustrations and gift. For ages 7 and up.

The Heart Way, by Deborah Rozman

The Heart Way is for children ages 6-12, although many adults and older children with a childlike spirit will enjoy the poetry, music, narration, and fun, practical heart games offered on this tape. The tape helps children *find* and *feel* the magic of their own heart power. From the heart, life looks different, problems are resolved more quickly, imagination is sparked and love flows. *The Heart Way* talks about attitudes and how your heart can change your life. Children are taught how to build heart power and make the magic in their life grow through appreciation and love.
$8.95, cassette, 25 minutes, repeats on Side 2.

Buddy Bubbles: Games for a Child's Heart, by Deborah Rozman

Buddy Bubbles is for children ages 2-6. Similar to *The Heart Way,* but geared to the understanding of a very young child, this tape helps children understand the difference between being in their heart and happy, and being out of their heart and fussy, angry or upset. They learn how to get in touch with their heart buddy whenever they need to and get real answers, and make the magic in their life grow through appreciation and love.
$8.95, cassette, 20 minutes, repeats on Side 2